Animal Kids
Cubs, Chicks and Pups

LEVEL **1** READER

Written by Kathryn Knight
Illustrated by Edizioni Larus S.p.A. and Sabrina Marconi

Little animal kids
come in all sorts of
sizes and colors.

Lynx cub

Some are
soft and fluffy.

Musk ox calf

Some are
not.

Rhinoceros calf

Lemur baby

Animal babies have
a mother and a father.
Many babies stay with
the mother until they
are older. Mothers
feed them and
hold them.

Orangutan
baby

Brown bear
cubs

Some animal kids
are called **cubs**.

Black bears, brown bears, and polar
bears all have cubs. Mothers teach them
how to find food. But what they really
want to do is play!

Lion cubs
stay with
the mother
for one
or two years.
A lick or a
kiss says,
"I love you."

Lion cub

Tiger cubs are born with
stripes—and very big paws!

Tiger cubs

Some animal kids
are called **pups**.

Seal pup

Seal pups and wolf pups make
squeak sounds when they need help.

Wolf
pup

Meerkat pups

Some pups live in tunnels under the ground. They come up top to play. When danger is near, they run back home!

Prairie dog pups

Some animal kids
are called **kits**.

Raccoon kit

A raccoon kit has little hands
that help it go up trees.
A fox kit has strong legs
that help it run and leap.

Fox kit

Some animal kids
are called **joeys**.
A joey is very tiny
when it is born.
As it grows, it stays
inside a pouch on the
mother's tumny.

Kangaroo joey

Some animal kids
are called **lambs**.
This little lamb
will one day grow
big, big horns!

Bighorn
lamb

Psst! Do you know what baby goats are called? They are called **kids**!

Mountain goat kid

Kids can walk on high mountain rocks.

Markhor kid

Some animal kids are called **chicks**. Chicks hatch from eggs. Hello, down there, little chick!

Flamingo chick

Many chicks grow
up in a nest.
The mother
or father bird
brings food
to the chicks.

Hummingbird
chicks

Some chicks learn to swim.
They also like to take rides!

Grebe chicks

Some animal kids
are called **foals**.

Zebra foal

A foal has long legs.
It can get up and walk
the day it is born!

Onager
foal

Some animal kids are called **fawns**.
Fawns have white spots. Little
fawns stay hidden in leaves or grass
while the mother looks for food.

Deer fawn

Some animal kids are called **calves**. A **calf** stays with its mother until it is grown.

Bison calf

Gnu (Wildebeest) calf

Calves can live
in the cold waters
of the sea.

Gray whale
calf

Calves can live
in the hot lands
of the desert.

Bactrian
camel
calf

Some animal babies
hatch from eggs.

A crocodile **hatchling**
calls out "Umf-umf-umf"
to tell its mother
it is hatching.

Crocodile hatchling

When she hears her babies,
she comes to dig the eggs
out of the sand.

Some penguin
fathers sit with the
eggs. When a little
chick hatches,
it stays close
to its father
to keep warm.

Emperor penguin chicks

Animal kids are busy.
They have bath time . . .

Elephant
calf

Cougar
cub

... lots of come-out-and-play time ...

Mara pups

... and rest
and nap time.

Hippopotamus
calf

Anteater pup

Some animal kids ride around
on the mother's back.
Hold on tight!

Gorilla baby

Sloth baby

Some animal kids ride around
on the mother's belly.
Cuddle up!

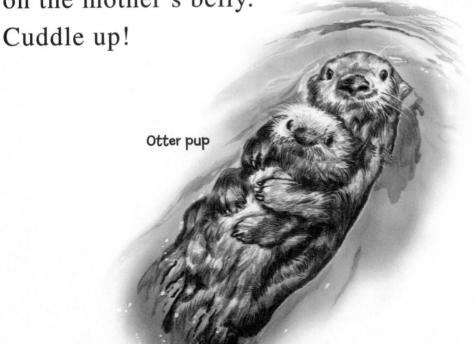

Otter pup

Manatee calf

When it's time to go to sleep,
some animal kids get
hugs and snuggles.

All tucked in?
Good night,
kids!

Great gray
owlet